Finding Your Way through the Gray:

A Guide to Positive Choices that Harness Your Potential

by
Michael Haynes

authorHOUSE™

1663 LIBERTY DRIVE, SUITE 200
BLOOMINGTON, INDIANA 47403
(800) 839-8640
WWW.AUTHORHOUSE.COM

First published by AuthorHouse 04/28/05

ISBN: 1-4208-4410-5 (sc)

Printed in the United States of America
Bloomington, Indiana

This book is printed on acid-free paper.

Acknowledgements

There are many people who have influenced my life in a profound way through our shared experiences and beliefs. It is appropriate to acknowledge, then, that their imprint is weaved among my own goals, aspirations, and beliefs. Among these influential people are:

My wife, Katherine

My parents, Jack & Shari Haynes

Friend and mentor, Coggin Heeringa

The people at Interlochen Center for the Arts

My friends and colleagues in East Jordan

My mentor and friend, Larry Pye

Table of Contents

Acknowledgements.. v
Introduction.. ix
I. What Is Gray?.. 1
II. Time... 7
    Moratorium on Negativity
    The "Only When" Whirlpool
    The Agony of Anticipation
    Fiscal Peace of Mind
    Set Goals
III. Tools.. 19
    Reciprocal Stimulation
    The 3 B's
    Wellness
    Activate Your Humor Radar
    Bridges
IV. Action 39
    Direct Your Day
    Take Risks
    Life Listing
    Choose Your Career, Don't Let it Choose You
V. The 4th B 57
Conclusion 61
Final Remarks 65
Bibliography 68
About the Author.. 71

Introduction

"Live out of your imagination, not your history." (Stephen Covey)

I first formulated the idea of "finding your way through the gray" a few years ago as I watched sleepy-eyed from my living room sofa the funeral of Princess Diana of Wales. I was amazed at the degree of mourning displayed over the loss. Her effect on the world seemed incomprehensible. I was jealous because, like most people, I knew that I would never receive such admiration and reverence at my funeral. It seemed unlikely that millions—even thousands—will want to pay their respects while the tones of a pipe organ echo through the mass. I am doubtful that anyone, save my immediate family, will recant stories of great heroism or re-read passages of my books. I am also relatively confident that, unlike Diana, statues would not soon be erected in my honor or ships christened with my name.

What became more and more evident as I listened and watched at 4:30 that day was that this person— who started off in a much less conspicuous life than when she ended—created extraordinary experiences. Like many great leaders in our world, Diana made conscious decisions every day to follow her dreams and persevered when life presented an unclear direction. So, although my life may not ever gain the degree of acclaim as other iconic figures, I am fairly optimistic that the way I approach the choices life presents me can have a profound effect on the quality and richness of my years ahead; Life is too short to waste time heading in the wrong direction and too precious to follow a direction prescribed by others.

The purpose of this book is to demonstrate that the world is a gray place—there is no single "right" answer—and that we all have the choice every day to create and harness our potential. Doing so—and approaching our days with this perspective—can enable us to live an extraordinary life.

1. What Is Gray?

"Intelligence is determined by one's ability to manage the gray" (Unknown)

In our world, there are countless prescribed rules that provide comfort and make our lives easier. Mathematical equations, laws that govern our society, computer programming language—are just a few. These things, widely referred to in context as "black and white," are just what they are…prescribed rules. However, life is a gray area. The choices we make about our words, actions, and beliefs are all open-ended. The people I have met in my life have proven that the gray area exists, and moreover, is either something to be harnessed or something to be feared. I suggest the former.

I once heard it said that "intelligence is determined by one's ability to manage the gray." This is very true—people who are able to live within the gray find connections where others might not. In his video titled Everyday Creativity, Dewitt Jones, photographer for the National Geographic, asserted that "there is more than one right answer…" The subject to which Jones was referring was the art of photography and, in a larger sense, being creative. In the video, he stated that it was possible to have the "right" perspective, the "right" focus, and the "right" lens. However, according to Jones, there is no single "right" answer when being creative.

A few years ago, I wrote an article for Principal Leadership, a magazine published by the National Association of Secondary School Principals. The article, titled "In the Gray" presented several scenarios that school officials face during the school day. The intent of the article was to provide examples of how "black and white" issues can be handled on a situation-by-situation basis using a touch of gray and how the resolution of these situations was better for the attempt.

The purpose of this chapter is simply to plant a seed—that the gray area is not something to be feared, and that it is not just about the pragmatics of life. Instead, if we approach the choices, words, and actions we are faced with a belief that life is a gray area...that life is not predetermined...that our reaction to the world is not prescribed...then we can be confident and successful knowing that everything can work out for our benefit if the right connections are made.

The World

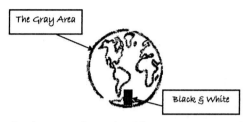

The diagram above should serve as a pictoral demonstration of the comparison between "black & white" and the "gray area."

Did you know... There's a real power in the gray. A friend of mine in the Army Reserves recently shared with me that the US military takes advantage of the gray—unlike many nations, the command structure of the US military enables officers at all levels to make decisions. Many of our foreign counterparts afford command privileges to only a few, and find themselves crippled if that person is taken out of the equation.

11. Time

"Day, n. A period of twenty-four hours, mostly misspent." (Ambrose Bierce)

 The average man has 3,900 weeks to live. That's 27,375 days, 675,000 hours, 40,500,000 minutes, and so on. I have seen larger numbers on television game shows and posted on state lottery billboards. Because our time is finite, maximizing our potential starts with making the most of <u>every single day</u>.

I recently attended a funeral in which the minister said (in reference to the deceased), "Larry was blessed when the doctor told him he had cancer." While an audible gasp was heard in the congregation, the minister went on to explain himself. What he meant was, that upon knowing his days were numbered, Larry was able to fast forward through all of life's unnecessary toils and make every day personally important. He learned to unfetter himself with the mundane, the ordinary, and the negative. Instead, he took advantage of the opportunity to squeeze the sweet nectar out of life <u>each and every day</u>. Larry made time work for him, and we can too.

Michael Haynes

Moratorium on Negativity

The first step is to institute a moratorium on negativity. In other words, stop allowing negative energy to consume what is already a finite amount of time. This concept applies to the choices we make about our attitude and the people with whom we spend time. Are we bummed about having to get up to go to work, or are we grateful for the opportunity to see our friends and colleagues? Are we dreading the morning walk, or are we geeked about being healthy and alive? Are we anxious about having to attend a party where we don't know many people, or are we excited to meet someone new? Are we willing to spend time with people who suck the life out of us, or do we gather with people who make us feel better and share their positive energy? Choosing the former in each of these examples keeps us headed in the right attitudinal direction.

The "Only When" Whirlpool

The second step toward maximizing our time is to appreciate time as an end to itself—not a means. "I wish the day would go by faster." "Everything will be better when this week is over." "When I get a new job, I'll finally be happy." These statements scream pathetic and imply a perspective that life's riches are separated by days or weeks. How miserable would life be if only some of our days had value? The "only when" whirlpool has the potential to drown us. Avoid it and make a vow to lose these words.

The Agony of Anticipation

*"Anticipation, anticipation
Is making me late
Is keeping me waiting..."
(Carly Simon)*

How many times have you been in a car and heard someone say, "How much longer until we get there?" What about the puzzling phenomena most of us have sensed that it seems to take longer going somewhere than returning? Similar to the "only when whirlpool" is the "agony of anticipation." A third step to making the best use of our time is to avoid the *agony of anticipation* at all costs.

This phenomena, like the "only when" whirlpool, is rooted in an idea that what lies ahead is more precious than the present. I don't want to dismiss the idea that some moments are more exciting... without them, life would be dull. However, it is important to keep everything in perspective and get the most out of <u>every</u> day.

The real danger is creating false or unatainable expectations. How many people do you know that create high expectations for future events, only to be disappointed when they finally reach the moment? The manic high lasts for a period of time, but always seems dwarfed by the low of the let-down.

A personal rule of thumb for me is to maintain a balance. Avoid preparing (mentally) for a trip until just before leaving. Plan for multiple high points or "peaks" when enroute. And most importantly do not shut off your other passions and vigor in anticipation of the destination.

Fiscal Peace of Mind

> *"Riches are chiefly good because they give us time." (Charles Lamb)*

Money cannot buy happiness, but it sure makes it easier! Maintaining a state of fiscal peace of mind is the fourth step to maximizing the quality of our time. The quote above, "Riches are chiefly good because they give us time" by Charles Lamb rings true. I love Lamb's remark because it can be construed in more than one way:

- Fiscal soundness affords us more leisure time.
- Time is less stressful when we are in a state of fiscal security.

It may seem out of place proposing that we should think about money in a book about making choices that harness our potential. After all, we have heard the familiar cliché, "money can't buy happiness" countless times. However, I truly believe that there is a comfort that enhances our life when we are fiscally stable.

I admitted this fact in the first year of my marriage. We were trying to sell our old house at the time and were fortunate enough to find a bank willing to lend us the money for a second home. Two mortgage payments, two car payments, college debt, and a fair amount of credit card debt were weekly—if daily—reminders that money was tight. As difficult as it was at the time, the lessons we learned about living fiscally well were significant. We learned that well-developed habits of budgeting and planning for the future can add a lot of peace of mind and decrease the stress that occurs when living paycheck to paycheck.

 So here is a gray area...faced with the paycheck to paycheck dilemma, create a budget. What appears depressing in the present will doubtless become more optimistic over time. A little saved each week adds up. The picture a few months away is more hopeful. Time creates hope, hope generates power, and with power is the choice to feel more comfort each day.

Bright Idea: Jot down a simple 3-column budget that lists income, expenses, and balance. Chunk it out for several months, being careful to list income conservatively and expenses liberally. Try to include everything you can think of. Over time, you should see the "balance" column grow. Remember, a little goes a long way and an extra $20 each paycheck can be hundreds by the end of the year.

Set Goals

The fifth and final step to making the most of our finite time is to set goals and take risks...to do something every day that stretches our minds or our bodies. This step will be explained in more detail later in the book.

III. Tools

"The most important single ingredient in the formula of success is knowing how to get along with people." (Theodore Roosevelt)

The chapter ahead presents a few new ideas that I would like to call tools. These "tools" are vehicles intended to stimulate our relationship senses and help us create or maintain positive interpersonal relationships.

Reciprocal Stimulation

The joy of telling a good joke for the *teller* is the laughter and energy of the response from the listener. The benefit of a compliment for the one giving it is the smile and appreciation returned in by the complimented. For the purposes of this book, my point, and the reader's enlightenment, I would like to introduce a concept called *reciprocal stimulation*. The only other place I have heard these two words used in concert were in a medical text involving cell growth.

Some words and actions, however, can also elicit a response from another that benefits the user. In this context, the phrase *reciprocal stimulation* should be used to describe the *response effect* of positive energy generated by people. It is an intangible energy can heighten the richness and texture of a moment.

From the time we wake in the morning until our head hits the pillow at night we each have countless opportunities to generate *reciprocal stimulation* from our words and actions. Examples include, but are not limited to the energy generated among:

- People involved in good conversation;
- People sharing in laughter;
- People involved in an exercise group;
- People participating in an athletic event

R*eciprocal stimulation* can also be applied to the way we live our lives. It is a recognized truism that success begets success. Major moments in our life, decisions, and acts can create within us a <u>drive</u> or <u>thirst</u> for even greater moments and more significant decisions or actions. In fact, our advancement as a species can be attributed in large part to the need to grow and learn and stretch ourselves.

Take, for example, the case of someone who makes a scientific breakthrough—the accomplishment undoubtedly feeds an internal need to continue to push forward; intellectual curiosity is stimulated and the work continues. The same scenario applies to athletes—the effect of endorphins and esteem that arise from an accomplishment tend to generate or renew a passion for reaching additional goals. How many marathon runners are satisfied after their first race?

The purpose of this point is to remind the reader that there is an energy within us that emerges when we expand our knowledge or skills, or when we share positive energy with others. Recognizing this as *reciprocal stimulation* not only helps us understand why we are driven, but hopefully reminds us that we each have a powerful role in the dynamics of life that can have dramatic benefits to ourself and others.

Bright Idea: Make it a goal to engage in a stimulating conversation with someone today. It might start with a statement such as, "I haven't had a chance to talk with you for a while... how have things been lately?" Make an effort to maintain eye contact and be interested. It is likely that the tables will turn and you'll be the one being asked, "How have you been?" or something similar.

The 3 B's

The *3 B's* is a second concept, or "tool," I would like to discuss before delving further into the chapters ahead. It is critical to the message central to this book—that we can make choices every day to harness our potential. In this case, I am referring to our potential to create genuine and positive relationships with other people. The *3 B's* stand for *be assertive, bedazzle*, and *be courteous*. The *3 B's* are things people can do every day in order to take charge of making their interactions with other people positive.

Be assertive implies an ability to initiate an interaction. For our purposes, *be assertive* will mean being willing to start a conversation with someone else. The conversation might begin by asking a simple question such as, "How was your weekend" or "How has your day been so far?" The dialogue might also start in the form of a compliment such as, "That's a nice shirt you have on today," or "You are really beaming...you must be having a great day." Being assertive can occur in nonverbal ways as well, such as a thumbs-up gesture or a pat on the back. Regardless, assertiveness is a critical ingredient to creating a positive interaction with others.

Bedazzle refers to our ability to charm. Being aware of our power to affect others' mood or situation by using facial expressions is helpful. *Bedazzle* is a nonverbal form of assertiveness that usually involves a smile or dynamic body gesture. When smiling or using facial expressions to *bedazzle* others, remember to lift your head and raise your eyebrows.

When I was in the sixth grade, one of my teachers taught me something that has stayed with me for nearly three decades. He challenged us one day to go home and make our mom feel good by offering a genuine gesture of appreciation. He reminded us that our parents had their hands full maintaining a household, raising a family, and working full-time jobs. Since Mother's Day was just around the corner, he suggested a few courtesies we could perform that would make our moms feel great. From that day forward, I have been thanking my mom every time she made dinner. It is a habit I still continue whenever I see my mom, and one that she recently mentioned.

It should be no mystery that the third "b" is *Be courteous*. It can mean helping or doing a favor for someone or being considerate of others' feelings, or having empathy. *Be courteous* is certainly not least important part of the *3 B's*, and little courtesies like the example above can genuinely have remarkable effects for the recipient *and* the giver.

The *3 B's* stand for three simple things anyone can do to generate and sustain positive interpersonal relationships. Being aware of the *3 B's* can be a powerful tool in this task.

Wellness

"A sound mind in a sound body is a short but full description of a happy state in this world."
(John Locke)

In order to maximize our ability to influence others and make positive choices about our life, I would like to discuss the concept of *wellness*. The concept of *wellness* is not original to this book. Usually used to describe a state of "balance" among various life aspects, the concept actually originates from an ancient Greek ideal that the mind, spirit, and body are all linked. With that in mind, this section focuses on physical wellness—and the understanding that physical wellness is critical to our ability to maximize other attributes such as our mind and spirit.

It is a proven fact regular exercise has a significant effect on our physical and mental wellness. Countless studies have shown that people who raise their heart rate through daily exercise regimens experience benefits including, but not limited to: weight loss, muscle toning, and happiness associated with increased endorphin levels. Physical wellness is more than being in shape, however. While being in good condition is a significant component, physical wellness implies a combination of overall body health and having a good self image.

The greatest point I would like to make here is about perspiration...sweat. It is my experience that sweating every day through exercise is the fastest and most substantial way to achieve physical fitness. Recently I heard a statement that rang true to me—that diets are short-term treatments for obesity and poor health. A more effective way to achieve physical wellness is to choose one part of our lifestyle and make a change. The change I suggest is to sweat more.

Let's think about the math. A pound of weight is roughly equal to 3500 calories. If we change absolutely nothing about our eating habits—caloric intake and fat content—but schedule time to burn off 500 calories each day, then it is a reasonable assumption that weight loss will follow. Burning an additional 500 calories would almost guarantee a pound of loss per week—4 pounds in a month and 52 pounds in a year. Although these numbers are loose and change from person to person, they nevertheless demonstrate the impact a few minutes a day can have on our physical wellness.

 Bright Idea: There are countelss books and websites that list various activities and the number of calories that can be burned for a period of time engaged in those activities. While the figures are generalized and vary from person to person, they are nonetheless helpful as a guide.

While weight loss is a very common topic relating to physical fitness, it is not the only issue. Regular exercise—sweating more and maintaining a healthy lifestyle—also has a dramatic effect on cardiovascular health, attitude, and even our self image. I have heard countless motivational speakers and people in the counseling profession report "…in order to be a positive influence on others, or in order to care for others, we first must take care of ourselves." It makes sense, then, that aspiring to achieve physical wellness is critical to our ability to positively influence others. Good self-image contributes significantly to charisma, attitude, and stamina.

"Time and health are two precious assets that we don't recognize and appreciate until they have been depleted." (Denis Waitley)

Bright Idea: Want to lose a few pounds? Eat too much at Thanksgiving? Easter? The holidays? Choose an activity that makes you sweat and vow to do it 30-60 minutes a day. Take a day off once a week to recover. Wait a few days and see if your jeans are any looser. When it works, you'll be so excited that you will want to keep going. Find a friend to exercise with...peer presure is powerful in the sweat business.

Activate Your Humor Radar

"As far as we know, laughter has no negative side effects--unless of course you just had an appendectomy" (Kevin Smith)

Laughter is good for our health. It makes us feel good. And it makes others feel good. A dose of humor has the power to change dull situations to exciting and uncomfortable ones to pleasant. Laughter can be a coping mechanism for dealing with difficult issues and it can have health benefits. Physically speaking, the benefits of laughter include, but are not limited to:

- A reduction of stress and tension;
- An increase in circulation;
- An increase in the immune system;
- An increase in mental alertness

In addition to advantages listed above, laughter is also a significant tool for fostering positive relationships. Laughter can form a connection between people and establish common ground. This brings me back to the concept of *reciprocal stimulation*. Humor is not only for the benefit of the listener, but the verbal and nonverbal cues associated with the response also benefit the person executing the joke.

A few years ago, I participated in a motivational workshop based on a program titled, <u>Fish! Catch the Energy. Release the Potential</u>. Among other concepts, one example featured the employees at Pike Place Fish Market in Seattle. The program spotlighted the way in which the employees at Pike Place Fish Market made work fun for both themselves and their customers, and demonstrated the power of the *humor radar*.

The workshop proved for me that, by using humor, it is possible to change what has the potential to be a dull, if unpleasant work environment to make exciting. A similar benefit can be attained by anyone, who regularly uses their *humor radar*. And it is not limited to the work place—it can be used at home and in social settings.

Humor can come in many forms and in many degrees—from subtle to hysteria. Both forms of humor can have a lasting effect. It is all about making the choice to provide others with positive energy and being willing to receive it in return.

"Cheerfulness is the best promoter of health and is as friendly to the mind as to the body." (Joseph Addison)

The list below contains a few examples of simple things anyone can do that shares humor to others.

Create your own words.

Tell people their shoe is untied when really it is not.

Dress for the holiday—St. Patrick's Day, Easter, Christmas, etc.

Keep a quarter in your pocket and give it to someone for no reason.

Share funny observations.

Wink at someone for no reason at all.

Smile at people.

Give someone a high five for no reason.

Make up a silly contest for people at work.

The list goes on.

 Bright Idea: Is there a holiday coming up? Start making up your own goofy jokes for the season and tell your friends, co-workers, and even your mother-in-law. They might laugh at the jokes, at you, or both. It is not likely that you will lose friends. It is likely, however, that you'll make someone's day.

Bridges

I like to think that we all have an erector set. Let me explain…Every day we are thrust into situations in which we have to confront or criticise someone, or offer difficult advice. The reason so many people avoid these situations is because they can be destructive. Words and thoughts shared freely can be hurtful, even if the intent is the opposite. The erector set to which I refer, however, is our ability to build bridges where once there might not have been.

Our erector set is made up of three things: style, vocabulary, and packaging. Style has to do with our inflection and body language, or deameanor. Feelings of being attacked or criticised can destroy bridges and prevent the message from being received. Leaning forward, maintaining eye contact, and speaking softly are ways to keep the listener attached to the conversation.

Vocabulary involves usage or composition of words. "Wow, that was sort of yucky.." The use of the word yucky in a tense situation is a good way to lessen the tension. "Hey, I'm comin' after you if you do that again." Executed with confidence, this statement establishes the problem while maintaining a connection through the campy approach.

Packaging is also critical in the bridge-building process. This does not mean to sugar-coat your comments. Instead, packaging refers to presentation. I like to use the sandwich approach whenever confronting someone on a particularly tough issue. That is, sandwich the criticism or comment between two positive ones. I like this approach because it allows the receiver to maintain a sense of respect and avoids a wall going up before the message is heard. Below are a few examples:

"I really liked the way you pulled Joe aside in private to discuss that matter. I was concerned that you were being a little harsh. But I think he knows that you care about his work."

"I know that looking professional is important to you. I am not sure jeans were appropriate yesterday. If you can always try to dress like you are now, that would be great because you look marvelous."

"Thanks for doing all of the laundry, I really appreciate it. Can you remember not to dry my

jeans the next time? I am fortunate to have someone to take care of me like you do."

Whether speaking to a friend, colleague, family member,or child, using your erector set can build bridges.

IV. Action

"The undertaking of a new action brings new strength." (Evenius)

"To be different you have to do something different." (Unknown)

According to John Dewey, "the self is not something ready-made, but something in continuous formation through choice of action." It is appropriate that this quote frame our perspective as we discuss actions.

The pages prior to this explored the benefits of using a set of tools to develop positive relationships. Using these tools can have a significant effect on the quality of our life directly or, in the case of reciprocal stimulation, indirectly. The pages ahead are about choices. Choices that, according to Dewey, have the power to define who we are...or who we will eventually become.

Essential to this power of choice is to have a plan. And choosing direction, whether it involve a specific action or choices related to major life decisions or directions, is an ultimate gray area. This chapter identifies a few action items that, when using the tools identified earlier, can dramatically enhance our life. The actions include *Direct Your Day, Take Risks, and Life Listing, and Choose Your Career.*

Direct Your Day

I have already made the point that finding your way through the gray and harnessing your potential begins by taking advantage of every single moment. By *directing your day*, I am referring to the notion that every moment has potential and whether we harness the power to make it positive, negative or neutral is a conscious choice we have to make.

It is important not to confuse being a *director* with being in a leadership role at all times. Most people—and good leaders—maintain a balance between times when they allow others to take charge or handle the reigns themselves. The former is a conscious decision that is a good example of *directing*. Directing your day, then, is intended to describe our ability to choreograph intrinsic and extrinsic energy and get the most out of every moment.

To continue identifying what it means to "direct your day," I will generalize our words and actions as being those of a *director* or a *follower*. In general, *followers* tend to live worry-free, uncomplicated lives. *Followers* wait for the scene to be set in social situations. They often respond to what others say and do and seldom initiate anything that could cause positive stimuli or *reciprocal stimulation*. *Followers* allow circumstance to dictate their feelings and reactions, and are comfortable being standers by in most instances.

Directors are people who take charge and create their own energy. *Directors* are quite the opposite of *followers*. *Directors* aggressively seek out opportunities to stimulate others. Consequently, they are more likely to receive positive energy (*reciprocal stimulation*) in return. To further strengthen my assertion, I would like to share a little about someone I know. For the purpose of my example, and to avoid any hard feelings, I will call him Ted.

Ted is a nice enough guy. He comes to work on-time every day and consistently executes his job. Step by step, he is meticulous and sticks with a routine that has worked for him for years. During a typical day, Ted has the opportunity to interact with as many as a hundred people. But Ted seldom initiates conversation. In fact, Ted hardly says anything at all unless required as a response to someone's query. If someone were to ask, "How are you doing today, Ted?" his response would be "Alright, (long breath), I suppose," or "I'm doin'." Many of the conversations in which Ted engages are similar—mostly reactive, never stimulating.

Ted, in this example, is a *follower.* Other conversations with Ted would lead you to the same conclusion. He can always be counted on to respond, but never initiates a conversation unless out of necessity. Ted, like many people, has fallen into the realm of submission—being willing to be a passerby in life. Unfortunately, this follow-the-leader attitude can easily become habit if gone unchecked for too long.

If Ted were to ask my opinion—and I assure you that he has not—I would suggest he turn over a new leaf and try to be a *director* rather than a *follower*. To be a *director*, Ted needs to turn on his tête-à-tête radar and grab hold of opportunities to initiate conversations. He might feel uncomfortable at first, but going out of his way to compliment a co-worker or inquire about someone else's day or weekend will begin to generate *reciprocal stimulation*. Because Ted is *participating* in creating the positive energy, he will be looked upon in a whole new light. By thinking of the *3 B's* (*be assertive, bedazzle, be courteous*), Ted can take a huge step forward.

I recommend that Ted think about all of the people he sees during the day and make an oath to initiate a conversation with at least three. It is a good idea if Ted were to come up with a question he might ask—one that could lead into a dialogue. Brevity is critical—30 seconds or so at first. A sudden change in Ted's personality could be dangerous, if scary, to his colleagues—not to mention his continued employment. Ted must also practice every day to lift his head high, raise his eyebrows, and smile when he greets people. Because Ted has struggled in the past fostering or creating positive interpersonal relationships, he may need to choose only a few people a day to try this out on. Finally,

I recommend that Ted look for opportunities to go out of his way to do a favor for 2-3 people each day. By thinking about the *3 B's* and remembering to *be assertive, bedazzle, and be courteous,* Ted will begin to experience reciprocal stimulation.

Another example I would like to share is a young married couple, who are followers—at least until they read this book.

On a particular morning, the couple wakes—both groggy and waiting for the day to greet them. A few words, no, grumbles, escape their lips almost incoherently. They continue with their morning routines, as if waking life were an inconvenience. Both of them respond to every moment as they reach it—decisions about what to eat, what to wear, and whether or not to turn on a radio or television. Needless to say, it seems that this couple has a mediocre—perhaps miserable—experience each and every day. As dull as the morning described appears to be, the couple is not without hope. Should both take an oath to become *directors,* their mornings—and days—will be much fuller.

This couple, as *directors,* has the opportunity to create their own type of day. With a little effort, energy can be unleashed and begin to spiral through the house. The *reciprocal stimulation* affecting each partner and is limitless. Following the same advice as our friend Ted, the couple would benefit by paying attention to the *3 B's*.

First of all, they should *be assertive* as they start their day. This can happen if both of them try to be the first one to greet the other in the morning. They can do this by making simple positive comments such as, "You look rested today," or, "How did you sleep?" While these questions seem simple, they set a positive tone for the start of the day.

Good facial expression is also important as the couple attempts to *bedazzle* one another. Not thinking about this could inadvertently cause tension between the two. Subtle cues of affection, a smile, or a hug go a long way to making someone feel wanted and cared for.

Finally, the couple in the example should look for opportunities to *be courteous*. Being courteous in their situation might be giving the other space if he/she is ill, offering to make breakfast for the other, or offering to get the newspaper or clean the dishes.

Ted and our couple are good examples and serve to solidify the vast difference between being a *director* or a *follower*. Should each of them aggressively seek opportunities to employ the *3 B's*, it is doubtless that they will maximize their potential for positive relationships.

I am excited to report that, since originally writing this chapter, Ted's directing has improved. The changes that have occurred in Ted's persona can be directly attributed to reciprocal stimuli. If you recall, Ted rarely initiated a conversation and some would describe him as glum. The author of this book made it a priority to engage with Ted in a conversation every day. Slowly, Ted began to laugh and sustain a conversation. Now, I am happy to say, he regularly initiates conversation and humor.

Take Risks

"Do something that scares you every day."
(Eleanor Roosevelt)

Life has flavor and should be tasted. We learn from our experiences and the more robust they are, the deeper our appreciation and growth from those experiences become. The bruises and anxiety that come with risks and challenges of doing something new or different serve only to heighten the euphoria of accomplishing something once thought possible.

Eleanor Roosevelt's quote, "Do something that scares you every day," is a great axiom; stretching your limits every day has benefits that are unimaginable and priceless. The quote hangs over my door and reminds me each day to stretch myself. Whether it is dealing with a difficult employee, calling an upset customer, or performing a challenging physical act, it reminds me to avoid operating in the "comfort" (more appropriately described "danger") zone.

A few years ago I learned how to snowboard. I thought myself mad at the time—I had tried to learn a few years before and had a miserable experience. I had read Eleanor's quote and was mystified, if jealous, of the students with whom I

 worked who were telling tales each Monday of their weekend adventures at "the mountain." The idea of careening downhill strapped to a wooden platform was definitely scary, but something in the back of my mind kept telling me that it would be exhilarating and rejuvenating to experience snowboarding myself.

The first day out was amazing! I had worked out in my head how I was going to stand, turn, and stop. As if guided by invisible hands, I managed to do each after a short time. Sure, I had a few knocks and falls and hurt knees...but I did it. My legs had never been so tired and sore.

The sensation at the conclusion of my first day at the mountain was so intense I could not get enough. I kept working on my snowboarding—always looking for more challenges like tricks and jumps. But in addition, I began to seek—no—thirst—for other opportunities to push myself. First, it was by running races, then, a marathon. There was no stopping me.

There are many people in our world who have had similar, life changing experiences because they were willing to take a risk. What is more important, however, is recognizing that life presents us with these opportunities all the time—risk-taking can occur almost anywhere. In addition to physical risks, opportunities to take risks often occur at the work place and in social scenes. Choosing to confront a difficult employee, making a stand for a principle, and asking for a raise are a few career risks. Asking someone out for the first time, proposing marriage, and telling others something personal are examples of personal risks.

Whether taking a risk involves personal, career, or physical boundaries, my suggestion is to take Eleanor's sentiment to heart. There are countless opportunities for us to face scary situations. Avoid being a passerby when these choices come along.

 Bright Idea: Is there something you've always wanted to accomplish, but did not take the time to do? Is there something you would like to try that is a little scary, like bungy jumping or sky diving? Choose one thing and make it a personal goal to accomplish it before the end of the year. Check-out books or web sites that explain the activity. The more you know, the more likely that you won't be so fearful.

Life Listing

Lists are great things. We use lists to organize our lives. We make lists before going grocery shopping. We make lists of people we want to remember at the holidays. Lists help us avoid redundancies at work or at home with the chores. Unfortunately, most people don't make lists for the most important reason—to live a rich and robust life.

Life listing is a term I would like to associate with the regular action of maintaining a *life list*. Such a *list* should include significant experiences you would like to have before leaving this world. It might include places you would like to visit, activities you would like to do, people you want to meet, a career goal you would like to meet, or any one of countless challenges and opportunities life has to offer.

I first created a *life list* as a high school senior. It was somewhat of a spoof. I was required to create it and did not take it too seriously at the time. That original list contained maybe ten or twelve items. Since then, I have heard the term *life list* used by friends, teachers, and in other books. I have also since rejuvenated my list to include real, attainable aspirations.

For me, maintaining my *life list* has become addictive and almost habit. The list on the next page is my own life list. It includes some of the items on the original, ten-item list, as well as the additions and changes I have made each year.

Bright Idea: Make your list organic. That is, when creating your own life list, it is important to remember that your dreams and aspirations will change or grow over time. It is also healthy to revisit the list ocassionally and change or add additional items. New Years is a good time to review the list. I recommend that listers have 5-6 new "resolutions" each year—some that are on the original life list, some that are new and have been born out of other rich experiences along the way.

My Life List

Graduate from College and Earn a Masters Degree
Be a Band Director
Work at Walt Disney World
Publish Something

Hold a Public Office
Run 5K Race
Get married
Learn to Hackey Sack
Play the Harmonica
Learn to Swing Dance
Learn to Wakeboard
Learn to Snowboard
Visit all 50 States
Go to France and See the Louvre's
Learn Martial Arts
Go Scuba Diving
Go on a Cruise
Visit a Frank Lloyd Wright House
Run in Central Park
Learn to Sail
Shoot Free Throws @ 90% Accuracy
Learn to Fly Fish
Earn a Gold Medal
Learn a Foreign Language with My Wife
Compete in Mountain Bike Race
Finish a Marathon
Save $500,000
Retire @ 50 Years Old
Read 500 Books
Act in a Musical
Learn to Surf
Go Whitewater Rafting
Finish a Triathlon
Go Rock Climbing

Go to England and Scotland

So whether you want to read 100 books, ride in the space shuttle, climb Mount Everest, or simply retire before age 55, a list can keep the goal alive.

"Boredom is a matter of choice, not circumstance."
(Unknown)

Choose Your Career, Don't Let it Choose You

"Find a job you like and you add five days to every week."
(H. Jackson Brown, Jr.)

Choose your own path, and do not let it choose you. I am amazed at how many people I have met over the years that have jobs they dread going to every day. Sure, there are circumstances and hardships that make it necessary to work at something that is not necessarily a first choice. However, this is a perfect opportunity to use the power of choice and creativity that lies within the gray area.

 Look at entrepreneur Tom Mognaghan, founder of Dominoes Pizza, who started a nation-wide pizza chain with only a few hundred dollars. Over time, with perseverance, he amassed a fortune and a billion dollar empire.

It really comes down to being willing to follow your dream. I met a young man a few years ago who worked a third shift factory job. Following a dream to be a musician, he dusted off the guitar he played in high school and began giving private guitar lessons. Over time, his lesson schedule was so busy and lucrative he had to give up the factory job.

Another person I met in college was working her way through school working 40 hours a week at a fast food restauraunt. She had a real love for making arts and crafts and began to sell them at flea markets and craft shows. Pretty soon, all of her time outside of school was being used to create her trinkets. She graduated, but did not stop following her dream. Now she owns her own craft supply store and is doing very well working for herself.

What is important to remember is that we all have what it takes to succeed at the things in which we are interested and have passions.

 Bright Idea: Are you unhappy with your job? What about not being satisfied with your income? Either way, think of something that you enjoy doing as a hobby. List ways in which you can capitalize on that interest. Maybe it is creating your own holiday cards or ornaments. Perhaps it is teaching a lesson on a musical instrument or fly fishing. Make up cards or a sign and post it at the grocery store, laundromat, or in the newspaper. How cool will it be when you begin making money doing something you love?

V. The 4th B

"Honesty is never seen sitting astride the fence." (Lemuel K. Washburn)

Earlier in the book I discussed what I call the *3 B's—be assertive, bedazzle, and be courteous.* As powerful as these are, and as much emphasis I have tried to place on skills that enable us to harness our potential, none are as important as the *4th B—Be Truthful.* Because it is so important, it is worthy of a chapter unto its own. The *4th B* is about two things: Being truthful to yourself and being truthful to others.

Being truthful to yourself is important. Finding your way through the gray requires that we be completely honest with ourselves. Without doing so, or by clouding our thoughts with false impressions or beliefs, we eliminate the <u>need</u> to see things in other ways. Imagine that our minds are like computers. Lying to ourself or being reluctant to approach situations <u>as they really are</u> is like trying to process two very different programs simultaneously. Unlike computers, it is not possible for humans to be efficient with both.

Being truthful to others is also critical in order to successfully manage the gray. I have met a lot of people who fear the gray because of bad experiences they have had. Too often, "the gray area" can be a scapegoat for *wishy washy* behavior. Let people know where you stand and stand there. The big gray picture involving choices at work, at home, and about life's direction are already unclear. Failure to maintain personal integrity can become like a box closing in on you limiting the opportunity to live in the gray and harness your potential.

Honesty is the best policy…and living a life with that guiding principle is key to the idea of finding your way through the gray.

Conclusion

"To live is to change, and to be perfect is to have changed often."
(Cardinal John Henry Newman)

As humans, we are presented with choices every moment of our lives. Our actions, the relationships we maintain, and our path are all a gray area. Like the people described in the examples, nothing is predetermined, and the power to create extraordinary experiences lies within each of us. Whether we take advantage of these opportunities is a conscious decision.

The ideas in this book were intended to jump start our ability to make positive choices—choices that enable us to get the most out of our time, to use the tools available, and to put into action a plan. Using each of these affords us power and the ability to harness our potential!

Final Remarks

As I began the journey of formulating the thoughts that I have shared in this book, I was fortunate to have had many mentors. It is an irony that among each of the people I consider critical to the formation of many of my thoughts and beliefs, the one commonality they have shared is their passion for learning and their recommendation of a book that they believed was worthy of thought.

Below is a short list of those books:

H. Jackson Brown, Jr., Life's Little Instruction Book

Stephen Bach, Smart Couples Finish Rich

Stephen R. Covey, The 7 Habits of Highly Effective People

Sam Horn, Tongue Fu!

Sam Horn, Concrete Confidence

Joseph Ellis, American Sphynx: The Character of Thomas Jefferson

Bibliography

Dewitt Jones, <u>Everyday Creativity,</u> (St. Paul, MN: Star Thrower, 1999), VHS Recording.

Lundin, Stephen C., Harry, Paul and Christensen, John. <u>Fish! A Remarkable Way to Boost Morale and Improve Results</u>. Hyperion, 2000.

Shea, Richard. <u>Book of Success</u>. Barnes and Noble Books, 2004.

Monaghan, Tom. "How We Got Started." <u>Fortune</u>. 13 September, 2003. Accessed March 1, 2005 at: h t t p : / / w w w . f o r t u n e . c o m / f o r t u n e / print/0,15935,475582,00.html

Stay Tuned for future books by Michael Allan Haynes:

The Cumulative Effect:
Harness the Power

Moxie Is Not A Bad Word

Things You Never Thought
You Would Hear In School

About the Author

Originally from Lakeland, Florida, Michael Haynes now lives in East Jordan, Michigan where he is a middle school principal. Michael's writing career began when he was a band director and wrote a monthly article for a local paper. He continued to write professional articles for the *School Band and Orchestra Magazine, Principal Leadership Magazine*, and the *Michigan Middle School Journal.*

Printed in the United States
39215LVS00001B/172-189